ENERGY FOR THE FUTURE
ENERGY FROM ALGAE

by Clara MacCarald

FOCUS
READERS.

NAVIGATOR

WWW.FOCUSREADERS.COM

Focus Readers is distributed by North Star Editions:
sales@northstareditions.com | 888-417-0195

Produced for Focus Readers by Red Line Editorial.

Content Consultant: Jeremy S. Guest, Associate Professor of Civil and Environmental Engineering, University of Illinois at Urbana-Champaign

Photographs ©: Shutterstock Images, cover, 1, 4–5, 7, 8–9, 11, 12–13, 15, 17, 19, 20–21, 22, 25, 26–27, 29

Library of Congress Cataloging-in-Publication Data
Library of Congress Cataloging-in-Publication Data is available on the Library of Congress website.

ISBN
978-1-63739-057-3 (hardcover)
978-1-63739-111-2 (paperback)
978-1-63739-214-0 (ebook pdf)
978-1-63739-165-5 (hosted ebook)

Printed in the United States of America
Mankato, MN
012022

ABOUT THE AUTHOR

Clara MacCarald is a freelance writer with a master's degree in ecology and natural resources. She lives with her family in an off-grid house nestled in the forests of central New York. When not parenting her daughter, she spends her time writing nonfiction books for kids.

TABLE OF CONTENTS

CHAPTER 1

TROUBLE IN THE WATER

For years, Roberts, Wisconsin, had a wastewater problem. Wastewater is water that people have used. The village treated its wastewater to clean it. Even then, too many **nutrients** remained. The water ended up in local lakes and streams. There, those extra nutrients could lead to toxic organisms taking over.

At wastewater treatment plants, dirty water from sewers is collected and cleaned. The clean water is reused or dumped into natural waterways.

In the early 2020s, the village tried an unusual idea. It used **algae**. A company set up a large greenhouse. Inside, the treated wastewater and algae flowed through tubes. The algae used the extra nutrients to grow. They removed the nutrients from the water.

The system was designed to clean more than 150,000 gallons (568,000 L) of water each day. It could grow nearly 100,000 pounds (45,400 kg) of algae in one year. Those algae could remove roughly 183,500 pounds (83,200 kg) of **carbon dioxide** (CO_2) from the air. CO_2 is a greenhouse gas. That means it traps heat in Earth's atmosphere. Greenhouse

Algae take in CO_2 from the air to make food.

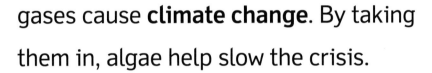

gases cause **climate change**. By taking them in, algae help slow the crisis.

Algae can help slow climate change in another way. People can make fuel from algae. The fuel is cleaner than other fuels.

Scientists studied Roberts's wastewater system. Someday, people everywhere could use algae to clean wastewater. Then they could use the algae for energy.

CHAPTER 2

A HISTORY OF ALGAE FUEL

During World War II (1939–1945), Germany ran low on fuel. Some German scientists tested algae as a source of oil. Oil can be burned as fuel. The scientists were unsuccessful. But in the 1950s, other scientists suggested making **biogas** from algae. In the 1970s, oil prices rose. Supply was limited. So,

During World War II, Germany's planes and tanks depended on steady fuel supplies.

scientists looked for new sources of power. They started making fuel from algae. But in the 1980s, oil prices fell. Interest in energy sources other than **fossil fuels** dropped.

Even so, research on algae continued. The US government had begun a program in 1978. The program studied the best ways to grow algae for fuel. Scientists tested different growing conditions. They tested different kinds of algae. But the price of algae fuel was much higher than that of other fuels. So, the program ended in 1996.

In the 2000s, people began worrying about limited fuel supplies again. They

A lab in the Netherlands researches the best methods of growing algae for fuel.

also grew more concerned about increased levels of greenhouse gases in the atmosphere. So, the US government again put money into algae studies. Companies also pursued ways to make algae fuel. But many companies gave up after a few years. The cost of making algae fuel was still too high. Research into lowering the cost continued.

CHAPTER 3

MAKING ALGAE FUEL

Algae are organisms that live in water. Like plants, algae make food with sunlight. They can also be grown for **biofuel**. But compared to plants, algae can make much more oil in the same amount of space. In addition, algae grow fast. And they can live in salty or polluted water.

Algae and other tiny organisms produce 50 to 85 percent of Earth's oxygen.

People can farm algae. To do so, algae farmers create ponds. Or they put water inside glass or plastic containers. Then the farmers add algae. They add nutrients. At harvest time, farmers use chemicals or air bubbles to clump the algae together. They remove the algae from the water. Then they make biofuel.

There are two main ways to make algae biofuel. Workers can add lots of heat and pressure to the algae. The result is oil. This process is similar to what happens underground to make fossil fuels. But making fossil fuels takes millions of years. People collect the oil made from algae. Then they clean it.

The second method of making algae biofuel is letting tiny organisms break down the algae. Different processes can

MAKING ENERGY WITH LIGHT

Algae make glucose from sunlight through a process called photosynthesis. Glucose is a kind of sugar. Algae use this sugar as a source of energy.

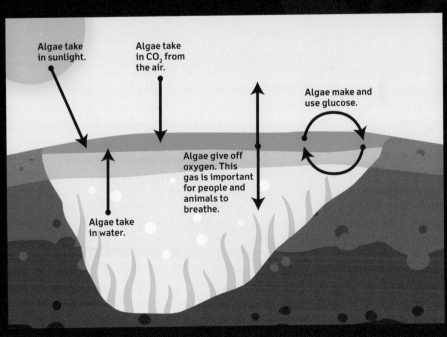

Algae take in sunlight.

Algae take in CO_2 from the air.

Algae make and use glucose.

Algae give off oxygen. This gas is important for people and animals to breathe.

Algae take in water.

make **ethanol** or biogas. Burning either gives off energy.

Algae fuel is **renewable**. New algae grow to replace the old. Also, using algae fuel does not warm the planet.

SOURCES OF BIOFUEL

People need organic matter to make biofuel. Often, that means plants. Sometimes the plant matter is a waste product. For example, sawdust and potato skins can make biofuel. Other biofuel comes from plant parts people could eat. Scientists are exploring nonfood sources of biofuel. Fast-growing trees are one option. Algae are another. These options have many benefits. They can grow on lower-quality land than crops. And they can improve the land's quality as they grow.

Burning coal releases extra CO_2 into the atmosphere.

As algae grow, they take CO_2 out of the atmosphere. When algae fuel burns, that same CO_2 returns to the air. So, burning algae fuel does not add extra CO_2 to the atmosphere. In contrast, burning fossil fuels releases CO_2 that hasn't been aboveground for millions of years. The extra CO_2 warms Earth. It causes climate change.

BIO INTELLIGENT QUOTIENT

The Bio Intelligent Quotient (BIQ) house opened in Germany in 2013. The house has 15 apartments where people can live. The BIQ was the first building in the world to be partly powered by algae. The algae live on the building itself.

Panels hold the algae. The panels are on the east- and south-facing sides of the building. These sides get the most sunlight. Nutrients and CO_2 mix with the algae. The algae grow.

A machine harvests the algae. The algae go to a small power plant inside the house. There, tiny organisms break down the algae. The organisms make biogas. The biogas burns. It provides energy for the house.

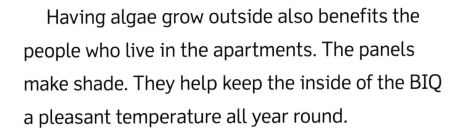

The BIQ house has 129 bioreactors. These glass panels offer algae a controlled environment in which to grow.

Having algae grow outside also benefits the people who live in the apartments. The panels make shade. They help keep the inside of the BIQ a pleasant temperature all year round.

CHAPTER 4

PROBLEMS IN THE PROCESS

Algae fuel has great promise. But it's not a practical energy source yet. Cost is the biggest problem. Fossil fuels are much cheaper. Algae fuel can't compete.

It takes a lot to grow algae. Growing large quantities requires vast amounts of water. Plus, algae need nutrients. They

Regular

$2.549

Some gas stations offer fuel that is 10 percent ethanol. Regular cars can't run on ethanol alone. So, the ethanol is mixed with regular gasoline.

Algae are mostly aquatic, which means they mostly live in water.

need sunlight and CO_2. In human-made systems, people must meet those needs. Also, making biofuel requires lots of energy. Some methods use more energy than the biofuel itself can provide.

There are ways to improve the growing process. People can control growing conditions. For example, they can grow algae in clear boxes. The boxes can be moved during the day to catch more sunlight. Or people can use wastewater. Wastewater is cheap. And it can provide algae with nutrients. The algae can even clean the water. Additionally, people can collect algae from the wild.

People are also improving the process of making biofuel. For example, different kinds of algae make different amounts of oil. Using the correct kind could help lower costs. So, scientists are testing how different algae perform.

Drying and processing algae requires a lot of power. Scientists are exploring new methods to reduce costs. In 2019, scientists tested a jet mixer. It separated oil from wet algae using less energy than other methods.

Finally, making biofuel creates waste. Some waste could be sold. It could be used in products. For example, pet-food

KINDS OF ALGAE

A species is a group of individuals that can breed together. The term is hard to apply to algae. Many small algae don't breed. They reproduce by splitting instead. Scientists may call similar algae the same species. But algae that look alike might have different genes. So, scientists don't know how many species of algae exist. There could be as few as 30,000 species. Or there could be more than 200,000.

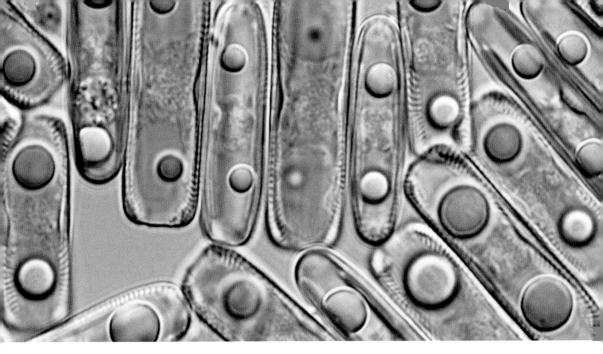

Some algae are diatoms, which live in Earth's soils and waters. Diatoms are key food sources for many animals.

makers use algae waste to make biscuits. Other companies make algae into a plastic. The plastic is used in shoes. People are finding ways to make money from algae waste. Doing so could help decrease the cost of algae fuel. Then more people could use algae fuel instead of fossil fuels.

CHAPTER 5

THE FUTURE OF ALGAE

Fossil fuel use is warming the planet. Using biofuel instead would lower the amount of CO_2 in the air. This move would slow Earth's warming. It would slow climate change.

Scientists are continuing to improve the process of making algae fuel. They are also exploring new uses for algae.

A biogas plant turns organic matter into fuel. Replacing fossil fuels with biofuel would help with the climate crisis.

Algae can remove CO_2 from the air. They can store CO_2 for long periods of time. And they can be made into products. These products also help store CO_2. The gas stays inside them instead of being released back into the air. With further

CAPTURING CO₂ WITH ALGAE

Burning algae biofuel returns CO_2 to the air. Scientists are looking at ways to store the CO_2 longer. One group discovered how to make carbon fibers from algae. The fibers have many uses. Tables, smartphone cases, and pens can be made from them. Building beams can be made from carbon fibers, too. The beams are as strong as steel. After use, the fibers can be buried underground. That way, the CO_2 in them never enters the atmosphere.

Many race cars use carbon fiber because the material is so lightweight.

research, algae could help with climate change. They could help power Earth's future.

FOCUS ON
ENERGY FROM ALGAE

Write your answers on a separate piece of paper.

1. Write a paragraph describing one way to produce fuel from algae.

2. Would you live in an algae-powered building? Why or why not?

3. Which fuel is not made by tiny organisms breaking down algae?

   A. ethanol
   B. oil
   C. biogas

4. Why would increasing the amount of sunlight algae get make the growing process more efficient?

   A. The algae would produce more ethanol.
   B. The algae would produce more biogas.
   C. The algae would grow faster.

Answer key on page 32.

GLOSSARY

algae
Tiny plant-like organisms that produce oxygen.

biofuel
A source of energy made from living matter.

biogas
A fuel in the form of a gas given off by matter that is broken down by tiny organisms.

carbon dioxide
A gas that contributes to global warming.

climate change
A human-caused global crisis involving long-term changes in Earth's temperature and weather patterns.

ethanol
A clear liquid that burns.

fossil fuels
Energy sources that come from the remains of plants and animals that died long ago.

nutrients
Substances that living things need to stay strong and healthy.

renewable
Having to do with natural resources that never run out.

TO LEARN MORE

BOOKS

Faulkner, Nicholas, and Jeanne Nagle. *Renewable Resources and You*. New York: Rosen Central, 2019.

Koontz, Robin. *Nature's Energy*. North Mankato, MN: Rourke Educational Media, 2019.

London, Martha. *The Energy of Tomorrow*. Minneapolis: Abdo Publishing, 2021.

NOTE TO EDUCATORS

Visit **www.focusreaders.com** to find lesson plans, activities, links, and other resources related to this title.

INDEX

Answer Key: **1.** Answers will vary; **2.** Answers will vary; **3.** B; **4.** C